Amazing Animals
Dolphins

James De Medeiros

WEIGL PUBLISHERS INC.

Published by Weigl Publishers Inc.
350 5th Avenue, Suite 3304
New York, NY 10118-0069

Amazing Animals series © 2009
WEIGL PUBLISHERS INC. www.weigl.com

Library of Congress Cataloging-in-
Publication Data

De Medeiros, James.
  Dolphins / James De Medeiros.
    p. cm. – (Amazing animals)
  Includes index.
  ISBN 978-1-59036-958-6 (hard cover :
alk. paper) – ISBN 978-1-59036-959-3
(soft cover : alk. paper)
  1. Dolphins–Juvenile literature. I. Title.
  QL737.C432D43 2008
  599.53–dc22

2008003758

Editor
Heather Kissock
Design and Layout
Terry Paulhus, Kathryn Livingstone

Photograph Credits
Every reasonable effort has been made
to trace ownership and to obtain
permission to reprint copyright material.
The publishers would be pleased to have
any errors or omissions brought to their
attention so that they may be corrected
in subsequent printings.

Cover: Getty Images; **Corel:** page 18;
Getty Images: pages 1, 2, 3, 4, 5, 6, 7,
8, 9, 10, 11, 12, 14, 15, 16, 17, 19,
20, 21, 23.

Printed in the United States of America
1 2 3 4 5 6 7 8 9 0   12 11 10 09 08

About This Book

This book tells you all about
dolphins. Find out where they live
and what they eat. Discover how
you can help to protect them. You
can also read about them in myths
and legends from around
the world.

Words in **bold** are explained in the
Words to Know section at the back
of the book.

Useful Websites

Addresses in this book
take you to the home pages
of websites that have
information about dolphins.

All of the Internet URLs given in
the book were valid at the time
of publication. However, due to
the dynamic nature of the Internet,
some addresses may have changed,
or sites may have ceased to exist
since publication. While the
author and publisher regret any
inconvenience this may cause
readers, no responsibility for any
such changes can be accepted by
either the author or the publisher.

Contents

Meet the Dolphin

Dolphins are friendly and smart animals that always seem to be smiling. They live in natural bodies of water around the world.

Many people confuse dolphins with fish. Dolphins are **marine mammals**. They breathe air just like humans. Every few minutes, dolphins rise to the surface of the ocean to breathe through a blowhole on top of their heads. The blowhole is always closed when the dolphins are underwater, but it opens when they come to the surface to breathe.

▼ Dolphins can hold their breath much longer than humans. They can stay underwater for more than 10 minutes at a time.

The Dolphin Family

There are 39 different kinds of dolphins.

- bottlenose dolphins
- common dolphins
- dusky dolphins
- orca dolphins
- spinner dolphins
- spotted dolphins

▲ The Atlantic spotted dolphin lives mainly in the coastal waters of southeastern North America.

A Very Special Animal

Dolphins have large tail fins called flukes. The front of each fluke is round. This helps dolphins glide through the water. The back of each fluke is flat. This helps dolphins push against the water. When a dolphin moves its tail up and down, the flukes push the animal forward. A dolphin's front fins are called flippers. Dolphins use their flippers to steer through the water.

▼ Dolphins can travel through water at speeds as fast as 25 miles (41.7 kilometers) per hour.

Dolphins use echolocation to tell what is around them. They do this by making clicking sounds. These sounds travel through the water. When the sounds hit something, an echo bounces back to the dolphin.

The blowhole is used for breathing. Dolphins keep the blowhole shut when underwater. They only open it to breathe.

The melon, located on the forehead, helps send underwater sounds.

The fin helps keep the dolphin balanced.

Flippers are used to steer the dolphin through the water.

A dolphin's teeth are cone-shaped with sharp points. They are used to grab and hold on to food.

The tail moves up and down. It helps the dolphin swim.

A Whistling Tune

Dolphins are very social animals. They are also known for being noisy. Dolphins make many sounds to communicate with each other. These include squeals, clicks, pops, yelps, and whistles.

Whistling is one of the dolphin's most unique sounds. Dolphins know many different whistles. Each dolphin has one special whistle, called its "signature whistle." This whistle may help dolphins tell each other who they are. Dolphins are also very good at imitating sounds they hear. They can even copy the signature whistles of other dolphins.

▼ A mother whistles to its baby, or calf, for several days after birth. This helps the calf learn its mother's signature whistle.

Dolphin Talk

- Dolphins do not have **vocal cords**. They make sound using muscles in their blowhole.

- Dolphins may use their bodies to communicate. They use many different motions, including shaking their heads and rolling over.

How Dolphins Eat

Dolphins eat squid, shrimp, sardines, smelt, herring, and many other small fish. They use echolocation to find food.

Dolphins sometimes work together to catch their food. A group of dolphins may surround and trap a school of fish. The dolphins then take turns feeding.

When a dolphin is about to eat, it grabs the animal with its teeth. It then swallows the animal headfirst without chewing.

▶ Shrimp are found in both the salt waters and fresh waters of the world.

What a Meal!

- Dolphins have three stomachs. Since dolphins do not chew, the stomachs help to break up the food before it is digested.

- Dolphins do not drink salt water from the ocean. They get most of their water from the food they eat.

▲ When hunting as a group, dolphins will sometimes push fish onto land, where they have difficulty getting away.

Where Dolphins Live

Dolphins are found in warm waters around the world. Most dolphins live in salt water, but some live in fresh water. Their three main **habitats** are in the open ocean, along the ocean coast, and in rivers.

During the year, dolphins move from place to place. Some move to warmer waters when winter arrives. Others follow fish that **migrate** with the seasons.

▼ Dolphins travel in groups called pods. The groups usually include adult dolphins and their children.

Dolphin Range

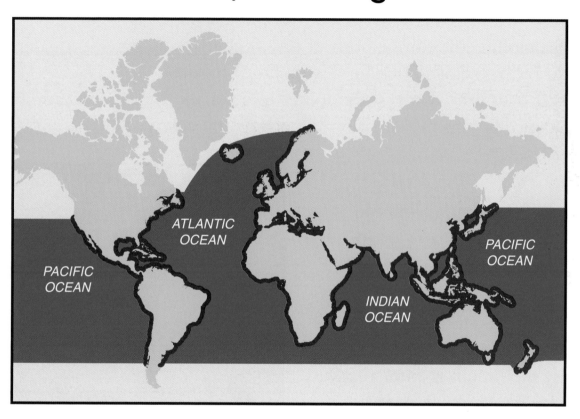

PACIFIC OCEAN

ATLANTIC OCEAN

PACIFIC OCEAN

INDIAN OCEAN

0 1,000 2,000 km

0 622 1,243 mi

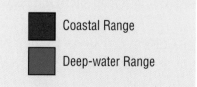

Coastal Range

Deep-water Range

Growing Up

A dolphin calf can be born at any time of year. At birth, a calf's back fin will be limp. It becomes stiff over time. Calves are darker in color than adult dolphins. Their color lightens as the calves get older.

A calf grows quickly. By the time it is four months old, a calf will be eating small fish. At age one, it will have its own signature whistle. A dolphin will leave its mother by the time it is eight years old. It will join a group of other young dolphins.

▶ Calves stay close to their mothers, but other dolphins, called "aunties," help watch over the baby.

Size Chart

Hector's dolphins are the smallest type of dolphin. They grow to 5.5 feet (1.7 meters) long and weigh up to 110 pounds (50 kg).

 Bottlenose dolphins grow up to 12 feet (3.5 m) long and weigh as much as 440 pounds (200 kg).

An orca, the largest type of dolphin, can grow to be 26 feet long (8 m) and weigh 8 tons (7 tonnes).

▼ The average dolphin lives between 25 and 30 years.

Friends and Enemies

Dolphins are friendly animals. They live together in small groups and help each other survive. They also share a bond with humans.

People fishing in the ocean have had dolphins help them gather fish. Dolphins also play with people who visit their watery habitat.

Humans have created problems for dolphins. Dolphins have died because humans have **polluted** the waters where they live.

▼ Sharks are one of the dolphin's few enemies. They will sometimes kill and eat dolphins.

Useful Websites
www.dolphinworld.net/
Dolphin-Behavior.html

Learn more about dolphin behavior at this website.

▲ Dolphins are often seen swimming near boats.

Living with Dolphins

There are many different animals that live in the same areas as dolphins.

- herring
- jellyfish
- sea turtles
- sharks
- smelt
- squid

Under Threat

The biggest threats to dolphins are water pollution and fishing nets. Both of these threats have injured and even killed dolphins. This has led to a decrease in the number of dolphins in the world.

Some types of dolphins are now **endangered** due to pollution and fishing. To save dolphins, countries are making laws that protect these animals from harm.

▼ Dolphins can become trapped in fishing nets.

Useful Websites

www.acsonline.org

Visit this website to learn about what is being done to protect and save dolphins.

▲ Industries sometimes pollute the waters in which dolphins live.

What Do You Think?

Dolphins are kept in sea parks around the world. They are trained to perform tricks and entertain people. Should dolphins be trained for entertainment? Should they stay in their natural habitat?

Myths and Legends

Stories about dolphins have been told for centuries. In most cases, they are described as helpful creatures. Some people even believed that dolphins were related to the gods. Others believed that they were related to humans.

Some of the earliest stories about dolphins are found in Greek myths. Dolphins protected and guided Poseidon, the god of the sea. His son, Triton, was half-man and half-dolphin. Arion, a Greek musician, was saved from drowning when a dolphin carried him back to land.

▶ Poseidon is often shown holding his trident. He used this fork-like tool to stir up the ocean waves.

The Chumash, an **Aboriginal** group from California, believe that dolphins were created from people who were drowning in the ocean. A goddess turned them into dolphins to save their lives. The Chumash treat dolphins as their brothers and sisters.

▼ Dolphins were featured on many coins from Ancient Greece. Sometimes, these coins were given to people as prizes at sporting events.

The Aboriginal Peoples of New Zealand and Australia also believed that humans and dolphins were related. They believed that their **ancestors** were dolphins who guided boats and rescued people.

Quiz

1. What do dolphins eat?
(a) **fish** (b) **meat** (c) **plants**

2. How many stomachs do dolphins have?
(a) **one** (b) **two** (c) **three**

3. What animals have been known to attack dolphins?
(a) **sardines** (b) **sharks** (c) **shrimp**

4. What is a dolphin's tail fin called?
(a) **flipper** (b) **fluke** (c) **melon**

5. What is a baby dolphin called?
(a) **calf** (b) **colt** (c) **kid**

Answers:
1. (a) Dolphins eat fish.
2. (c) Dolphins have three stomachs.
3. (b) Sharks attack dolphins.
4. (b) A dolphin's tail fin is called a fluke.
5. (a) A baby dolphin is called a calf.

Find out More

To find out more about dolphins, visit the websites in this book. You can also write to these organizations.

Dolphin Research Center
58901 Overseas Highway
Grassy Key, FL 33050-6019

**National Marine
Mammal Laboratory**
7600 Sand Point Way NE
Seattle, WA 98115-0070

**Whale and Dolphin
Conservation Society**
191 Weston Road
Lincoln, MA 01773

Words to Know

Aboriginal
original inhabitants of an area
ancestors
people from the past
endangered
at risk of no longer living on Earth
habitats
the natural environments where
a specific animal lives

marine mammals
warm-blooded animals that live in water
migrate
to move from place to place depending
on the season
polluted
made dirty
vocal cords
body parts that produce voice sounds

Index